SHORT WALKS AROUND – ST IVES

TOBI CARVER

Short Walks Around - St Ives

© Tobi Carver/St Ives Printing & Publishing Company

First Edition published 2009

Photography & Design: © Tobi Carver

Printed & Published by:
The St Ives Printing & Publishing Company,
High Street, St Ives, Cornwall TR26 1RS UK.

www.stivesnews.co.uk

ISBN 978-0-948385-48-0

INTRODUCTION

OVER THE YEARS St Ives has attracted millions of visitors to its streets and beaches, all drawn by the beauty of the town. People often quickly scurry through the town heading for the beaches or slowly amble the streets gazing in shop and gallery windows, but you miss a lot by not looking deeper, by not looking up. By looking above the first floor level you would see the interesting architecture of the town or catch a glimpse, through a gap in the buildings, of St Nicholas' Chapel on the summit of the Island. This book aims to help guide you through *Short Walks* but remember to look around and enjoy.

Mostly pleasant strolls in beautiful surroundings, the longest walk is Walk Fifteen, along the field-path from St Ives to Zennor (approx. 4 miles).

The Walks are divided into four sections. Section A consists of circular walks in and around St Ives which require no transport. Section B will take you on circular walks where transport is required to reach the start or from the finish. Section C contains five point to point walks requiring transport to reach the start. All five finish in St Ives. Section D contains more out-of-the-way walks where transport will be needed to reach the start.

Nothing is really required for any of these walks but do plan for the weather and carry the appropriate clothing and refreshments. A large scale Ordnance Survey map is worth having in case any natural feature catches your eye. The OS *Pathfinder* series is a good choice. Bus routes do run close to the start points of some of the longer walks – but check timetables as, especially outside of the tourist season, bus times become less frequent.

Enjoy the walks. Enjoy the atmosphere. But most of all enjoy the scenery which will range from the twisting streets of St Ives and its glorious beaches to the cliffs, hills and moors of the outlying areas.

LIST of WALKS

OLD ST IVES

START at the St Ives Parish Church which is situated in the Market Place, facing Market House. The corner opposite is the home of the town's war memorial with gardens behind – a pleasant place to spend a few minutes.

From the church turn right and follow the churchyard wall down Lifeboat Hill to the RNLI station at the root of West Pier. You are now on Wharf Road, St Ives' harbour front.

Follow the wharf as it tracks around the harbour towards Smeaton's Pier. The first building on your right houses the fishermen's lodges of Shore Shelter and Rose Lodge. Continue past the slipway to the Sloop Inn on the corner of Wharf Road and Fish Street. The next building on your right is the third of St Ives' fishermen's lodges. Shamrock Lodge is surrounded by a wall, a wartime defence, built in 1940 – it also serves to protect the structure from the sea.

Continue along the Wharf until you reach Quay House on your right and Pier House on the left. From here a rightward detour will take you along Smeaton's Pier. Towards the end, and after, the 1939–45 war members of the Royal Marine Commando Cliff Assault Wing were based in St Ives and at the beginning of the pier is a seating area which also boasts a plaque commemorating the Commando relationship with St Ives and its people. Opposite is the fishermen's chapel of St Leonards. The seating area overlooks the remnants of the old pier known as the 'Rampers'. Smeaton's lighthouse with it's squat walls and shiny coppella marks the end of Smeaton's design and the start of the Victorian Pier extension completed in 1890.

Back on the walk and following the road round, keeping the sea wall hard on your right, you will reach the town's Museum at Wheal Dream. A set of steps leads down on the right and round to a car park overlooking Porthgwidden Beach.

Follow the road out of the car park and head right. Cross the Island car park ahead of you and follow the roadway up across the slope of the Island itself, up to the National Coastwatch Institute's St Ives lookout. Follow the crest of the hill back along the ridge to St Nicholas' Chapel which dominates the Island's summit. Once here you can enjoy views over St Ives' main surf beach, Porthmeor. In the distance is Carrick Du, also known as 'Carthew' or 'Man's Head' (Walk Two) and further still to Clodgy Point (Walk Three) with its distinctive 'camel' shaped rock.

From St Nicholas' Chapel head down the hill along the obvious path but once on the flatter grass head rightwards to the corner of the beach where a walkway takes you to Porthmeor Road. Turn right and then right again into Back Road West. As you walk along Back Road West you will pass, first on your right, the Penwith Society of Artists building opposite the St Peter's Street Methodist Chapel. Further along on your left is Norway Square, in which stands the St Ives Society of Artists building, and opposite the St Ives School of Painting.

Continue until the road makes a ninety degree turn to the right leading to Porthmeor Beach. Turn left here and you are in the Digey. The Digey leads you to Fore Street where you turn right and follow the town's main shopping street back to your start point in the Market Place.

CARRICK DU

START as for Walk One at the Parish Church. Walk along Fore Street – how much time you spend depends on how much shopping you do! About halfway down the street is a set of granite steps rising steeply on your left, these are Academy Steps and will lead you to the completely hidden Academy Terrace. If you find yourself at a Chapel set back from the road, on your left, you have gone about thirty yards too far.

The steps bring you out towards the top of Barnoon Hill in front of a terrace of houses. Walk along the front of this terrace turning left at its end. Continue along the road in front of you with the car park on your right. The car park will give way to Barnoon Cemetery.

Follow the road alongside the cemetery wall and you'll reach Porthmeor Hill. Cross the road and walk past a few small shops. Take the first right which leads down onto Ocean View Terrace. Continue until the road branches, taking the left into Orange Lane.

Almost immediately you will see a block of flats on the left, just past which the road bends again to the right. Straight ahead of you is a small footpath which will take you down towards the coast path. At a junction

with a second footpath turn left and follow this new path to the main coast path. Once there a right turn onto the path will take you to the obvious headland of Carrick Du or Man's Head. The views from here are over Porthmeor Beach towards the Island and St Nicholas' Chapel.

For your return follow the footpath back towards Porthmeor Beach. The first road you reach is Beach Road and facing you, where it joins Porthmeor Hill, is Venton Ia, 'St Ia's Well'. The road will continue to lead you round, with the beach on your left, until you reach the top of the Digey.

From here finish as in Walk One. Straight down the Digey, right into Fore Street and down to Market Place and the Parish Church.

CLODGY POINT

START at Barnoon car park. After you have paused to take in the fabulous view over the Island and Porthmeor Beach walk along the road which follows the crest of the hill with the cemetery on your right. When the road meets the road up from Porthmeor Hill cross over and continue along the right hand side of the road. Continue along Ventnor Terrace, Wheal Ayr Terrace, Alexandra Row and turn right into Burthallan Lane beside signs to the Garrack Hotel.

Burthallan Lane itself peters out into a footpath which, after a little way, joins the Coastal Footpath at Clodgy Point. From here you will see the coast disappearing in a series of headlands and coves towards Zennor five miles away. A continued walk to Zennor is only recommended for the hardier walker, as it is tougher than you might think. If you choose to do this it is a good idea to check bus times as they often vary between seasons and days of the week.

Once you have finished enjoying Clodgy return along the coastpath to Carrick Du and onwards to Porthmeor Beach. Beside the cemetery at the Tate Gallery end you will find a ramp on the right hand side of the road leading to an expansive flight of steps which will return you to the Barnoon car park, or walk through the cemetery itself.

PORTHMINSTER POINT

START at the RNLI station on the harbour front. Walk along Pedn Olva or 'Lambeth' Walk beneath the wall of the Parish Church. At the end of the Walk continue up the Warren past the Pedn Olva Hotel. Just past the hotel on the left is a flight of steps which will lead you down to Porthminster Beach. When the tide is low the steps provide access to the beach and an alternative to walking along the roadway. Be warned the steps become rocks and can be slippery when wet. Where these steps start also provides the walker with their first view across Porthminster Beach to the Point behind.

Continue on and leave the road where a ramp on your left descends to the beach. Walk along the top of the beach to the Beach Cafe or, if you choose to walk along the sand, you should aim to meet with the coast path at this point. Past the cafe the path steepens.

Continue uphill and cross the bridge over the St Ives – St Erth railway branch line. As the hill steepens again you are walking through an area which was once a pleasure garden built on land donated by local shipping magnate, Sir Edward Hain. On the right hand side an outcrop of black rock is visible. Here, on the left, you will see a footpath leading off the main slope. Follow this path until you join a road. Straight ahead you will see some buildings and a bridge to the left. Cross the railway bridge and you will be on the grassy slope of Porthminster Point. From here you can pause and enjoy the views over the bay. Return the way you came.

The Hain Steamship Company

In a time when St Ives had a large fishing fleet, and several shipping companies, Sir Edward's, Hain Steamship Company dwarfed all others. Born in 1851, Sir Edward was the fourth Edward Hain and presided over the period which saw the greatest expansion of the company founded by his great grandfather in 1816. Starting with a fishing lugger the first Edward Hain expanded into cargo, shipping cured fish to the Mediterranean and returning with Greek and Turkish dried fruit. The acquisition of a schooner made trade possible in West Indian sugar and Brazilian coffee.

After several years in banking and commerce in London, Sir Edward, who had never shown a desire to go to sea like his forebears, saw the potential of steam. The company's first steamer the *Trewidden* was commissioned in 1878 from the Redhead yard in South Shields. This was the first of many as Redheads went on to build seventy-three more during Edward's lifetime and a total of eighty-seven ships were delivered by them. All vessels were identified by the prefix *Tre* and a large letter 'H' on the funnel.

Families of Hain ship crew members were kept up to date with ship movements with weekly columns in *The St Ives Times*. The fleet served through both World Wars, suffering great losses both in men and shipping. A few years after Sir Edward's death in 1917 the Company moved to Cardiff, later to be bought out by the London based P & O.

Sir Edward amassed a considerable wealth and, like his company, provided for members of the St Ives community. He funded the rebuilding of St Nicholas' Chapel on the Island and presented areas of land to the town as communal spaces, such as the Porthminster Pleasure Gardens. Perhaps the most important donation to generations of towns people was when the Hain company's board of directors funded the establishment of the Edward Hain Memorial Hospital as a permanent and functional memorial to Sir Edward's son, Captain Edward Hain who was killed at the end of 1915 during the Gallipoli campaign on the Dardanelle Peninsular, possibly amongst the groves that had provided the Turkish fruit of those early shipments.

HAIN WALK

START at the Parish Church but first take a few moments to look around the church and its yard which provides views over the harbour and bay. On the way out notice the 10 foot high carved lantern cross which was rediscovered and re-erected in its current spot beside the Church porch, in 1858.

From the church gate turn left into St Andrews Street which leads you up Skidden Hill. At the top, on your right, is the town's Roman Catholic Church where, if you found the hill a bit much, you can pause to rest on the bench, below an interesting plaque. Turn left on to Fernlea Terrace and follow the main road out of St Ives. All the way along you will see some of the best views of St Ives Bay. As you walk up the road you will pass the Porthminster Hotel and, further on, a row of white buildings below the level of the road. These were once the Coastguard Houses and from here you can see one of the town's most photographed views.

The Victorian and Edwardian houses you pass as you continue along the road reflect the prosperity of the town's industrial past. Grandly built they were the homes of mine engineers and captains (those in charge of the area's mines) and sea captains. Past the garage the road now straightens out for a while and here on your left is Treloyhan Manor – the grandest of these houses.

The Manor was built by St Ives' greatest shipping fleet owner, Sir Edward Hain. On the right of the road are the grounds and entrances to Tregenna Castle Hotel. The hotel, built as a private home by one Samuel Stephens, was purchased by the Great Western Railway in 1895 and has been used as a hotel ever since. Next you will see the Cornish Arms public house on your right.

Take the second left past the Cornish Arms which is the unpaved lane of Wheal Margery. Wheal Margery is actually situated near the old Margery mine, 'Wheal' being the Cornish word for mine. Follow Wheal Margery down until it forks. Take the right side of the fork and to your left you'll see a footpath and gate. Follow this narrow path and you'll reach Hain Walk.

At the footpath's junction with Hain Walk a path leads down right to Carbis Bay Beach, however, you turn left. Follow Hain Walk as it moves past the boundary wall of Treloyhan Manor and as you see the sea again, on your left is the Huer's Hut. From here a watchman 'the huer' would keep an eye on the waters of the bay for the tell-tale signs of a pilchard shoal. Once seen he would signal to the pilchard fishermen, and precipitate a frenzy of fishing which would involve the whole community, to surround the shoal and drive them ashore where the rest of the men and the women and children gathered the fish up for salting and packing.

A little way past the hut and the road turns leftward up a hill with a steep hill arrowing down straight ahead. Go on down the hill, through an area of land which was once a manicured pleasure garden, and over the metal railway bridge and down to Porthminster Beach.

Continue along the top of the beach and up towards the Pedn Olva Hotel. From the hotel you find yourself in the narrow street of The Warren. At the bottom of The Warren stands the St Ives Arts Club at Westcotts Quay. Keep to the sea wall along Lambeth Walk to the RNLI station.

Taking a left here will lead you back to Market Place.

WORVAS HILL & KNILL'S MONUMENT

START in Royal Square. Between the Western Hotel and the Cinema is Dove Street, follow this to the back of the Cinema where a ramp leads to the police station. A flight of steps beside the station takes you up to Park Avenue. Turn right and continue along the road. From here you may wish to pause and look out over the harbour and the Stennack Valley.

Before the road drops in height a car park is on your left with a pedestrian road-way leading up between the road and the car park. Follow this slope to the Trenwith Car Park. Walk through the car park past the Leisure Centre and into the field behind. Follow the track through the field and the farmstead of Bahavella, after which the pathway splits. Take the main left fork and continue until the roadway bends to the left and a footpath continues straight ahead. Follow the footpath. It will

become more of a roadway as you pass beside houses before meeting Trenwith Lane at the Belyars Bowling Club. Turn left and follow the road for fifty yards until you turn right, at the junction, into Steeple Lane.

Follow the road for about three quarters of a mile until you reach the top of the hill. Descend seventy-five yards and you will see an information board on the right and a path leading up to John Knill's Mausoleum. Continue up the path to the 'steeple' itself. Once within the precinct of the monument you will be able to enjoy the full view across the bay.

You now have two options. You may return to the road by the path you have just walked up. If so once at the road turn right and start off down the hill. The second and better option is to walk a little way back down the path before branching off on a smaller path and wandering down through the Steeple Woodland Nature Reserve. At the bottom of the Reserve you will meet a footpath. Turn left and you will rejoin the road and any of your friends who chose option one.

Continue down Steeple Lane and you reach the main St Ives road at the Cornish Arms public house. Return to St Ives along the main road.

John Knill

John Knill has provided St Ives with a unique ceremony. The quinquennial ceremony sees a fiddler and master of ceremonies lead two widows and ten little girls to Knill's mausoleum accompanied by the Town Mayor, Customs Officer and Parish priest. The ceremony follows a routine as prescribed in Knill's own will.

Johannes Knill was born in 1733 in Callington, South East Cornwall. After working for a firm of solicitors in Penzance he became the Collector of Customs in St Ives in 1762. At the age of only 34 he was elected Mayor in 1767.

His career continued and he was promoted to Inspector of Customs. It is also believed that William Pitt used Knill's legal skills to prepare Parliamentary Bills. In 1781 he became a member of Grays Inn and left St Ives to reside in the capital. This was a move he never returned from.

In 1782 Knill purchased Worvas hill for five guineas from John Arundel and the process of building his fifty foot high, three sided granite pyramid began, the pyramid is hollow.

Knill, however, was never placed in his mausoleum. He died, unmarried, in March 1811 and was buried in Holborn in London. Every five years the ceremonial procession arrives at the 'Steeple' which is opened every other quinquennial to allow those present to see inside his empty tomb.

AROUND LELANT

START at Lelant railway station. Walk along the road with the estuary to your right. When this road joins Church Lane at a triangle of grass, turn right and wander up to the church.

Follow the footpath down between the church and the graveyards, across the golf course and past a Second World War machine-gun pillbox, to the beach beside the estuary's channel. This beach will lead you leftwards onto Porthkidney Beach. Follow the beach as far as you want.

At several points you can break left up into the dunes where, cutting through them landwards, you will reach a fence line beside the railway. Turn left and follow this fence line until you rejoin the path beside the pillbox. Turn right the way you came and once back at the church head straight down the

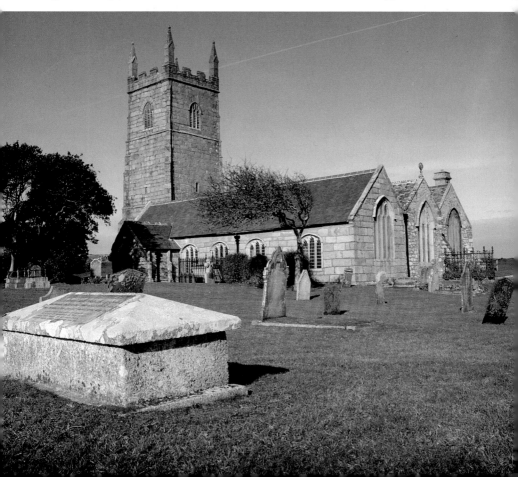

road with your back to the church. Continue past the road to the station until you arrive at the junction with St Ives Road opposite the village's small war memorial.

Turn left down the hill beside the Badger Inn, this will bring you back to your start point at Lelant railway station.

Lelant Church and the St Michael's Way

While today Lelant is just a small village, compared to St Ives, that was not always the case. In the early medieval period St Ives was in the parish of Lelant and its inhabitants were required to provide for the upkeep of the church, nestled amongst the dunes. In 1662 one naturalist wrote that the church was 'almost quite covered with sand blown up by the wind.'

One tradition states that the castle of Theodoric, King of Cornwall, lies beneath the sands at Lelant. In J.H. Matthews 1892, *History of Saint Ives, Lelant, Towednack and Zennor* he notes that:

> 'Norden says Lelant was 'sometyme a haven towne, but now of late decayed by reason of the sande which has choaked the harbour and buried much of the lands and howses; many devises they use to prevent the obsorpation of the churche.'

From the beach at Lelant to St Michael's Mount on the south coast lies the route of St Michael's Way, one of a network of pilgrim routes that stretch throughout Europe.

In medieval Europe one of the three most important Christian sites was that of the Cathedral of St James in the Galician town of Santiago de Compostela (St James in the field of stars) to which many pilgrims flocked. The St. Michael's Way was used by pilgrims, missionaries and travellers, sailing down the North coast from areas such as Ireland and Wales, to avoid entering treacherous waters around Land's End.

The town grew in fame as a site of pilgrimage as the church housed the remains of St James the Greater, the Patron Saint of Spain. One story says the Virgin Mary appeared to a young boy and told him where the body of James, son of Zebedee, lay after it arrived in Galicia following his death in the Holy Land.

St Michael's Way is just one section of the Way of St James and has been used since pre-history (10,000BC - 410AD). It is also thought that the way assisted in Cornwall's rapid conversion into a Christian faith.

The trail stretches from Lelant to Marazion and St Michael's Mount, thus stretching 12.5 miles/19.5 km. The trail can be found using the OS' Explorer 102 or Landranger 203 maps.

AROUND ST ERTH

FROM St Erth Church follow Chenhalls Road with the river on your left towards Hayle. Once you leave the village the pavement runs out so watch for traffic as you continue until the road bends sharply to the left. Just before the buildings a footpath leads off on the right. This footpath will bring you into a large field. Continue along the boundary until you reach a second footpath cutting straight across the one you are on. Turn right and follow this second path up the hill.

The path leads you through a cut into Trenhale Lane. Turn right and continue past the school, and into the village's main square. Here you will find the Star Inn where a board contains information about the St Erth Pits. The Pits are a Site of Special Scientific Interest (SSSI) for their significant addition to the fossil records.

Go straight across the road and down the hill until its junction with Green Lane. Turn left and follow the road past the coarse fishing ponds. The road will lead you to a bridge crossing the river Hayle. Once over the bridge you follow the flow down river, back to St Erth. As you approach the village you get a good look of the old bridge, which you cross, to return to the church for a look around its yard.

St Erth Church is one of the prettiest in the area. Dedicated to St Erth, the church was built on its present site around 1215, although an older church may have stood on the hill overlooking the village. Believed to be the Irish saint Erc of Slane, Erth was a brother to both St Uny and St Ia.

The churchyard contains a number of interesting stones and memorials nestled between its trees and shrubs. Among them is an enclosure (immediately on your left as you enter the church) containing the grave of six victims of an 1832 cholera outbreak.

Beside this is the village's war memorial. The grave of Major Herbert Augustine Carter VC, it was given to the village as a memorial by his wife Helen Lillian Wilmot Carter. Twenty-two feet high the memorial is a Calvary Cross, mounted on a stone plinth. The cross is flanked by two figures with the Virgin Mary cradling Jesus on its rear and bears both the Carter and Wilmot arms.

Twenty-three names from both world wars are listed on the plinth, including Carter's brother, Noel Conway Carter DCM of the 2nd South Africa Horse, who died in 1917 of blackwater fever while in Johannesburg. Carter himself died in 1916 having won his Victoria Cross in 1903 during operations prior to the Battle of Jidballi during the 4th Somaliland Expedition.

The son of the Rev. Conway Richard Dodds Carter, who for twenty-five years was St Erth's vicar, Herbert was a Lieutenant in the 6th Mounted Infantry of the Indian Army carrying out a reconnaissance to ascertain the strength of the 'Mad Mullahs' Dervish forces. The small group was sighted and forced to withdraw pursued by a Dervish force which outnumbered them thirty-to-one. During the withdrawal a Private, Jai Singh, was wounded and his horse killed. Carter rode 400 yards back to the Sepoy who was so badly injured it took three attempts to get him onto Carter's horse. During the engagements around Jidballi in December 1903 and January 1904 two VC's were won. Interestingly the second also has a Cornish connection being won by Lt. Clement Leslie Smith of the Duke of Cornwall Light Infantry. Lt. Smith, who rose to the rank of Brigadier-General, won his in a similar manner rescuing a medical orderly during the battle itself on 10 January 1904. Both medals are on display in the Duke of Cornwall's Light Infantry Regimental Museum in Bodmin.

By 1916 Carter was in Kenya, a Major in the 101st Indian Grenadiers. Suffering from fever he force marched his command two days to Mwelo Mdogo to relieve Mwelo's fort, besieged by German colonial forces. Too great an effort, Carter died of fever induced heat exhaustion on 13 January.

AROUND NANCLEDRA

THIS is a very simple walk which takes you down the Red River from Nancledra before swinging you up to the heights of Cripplesease and back.

From the bus stop in Nancledra head down hill along the road until you reach a lane leading off to the left shortly after the bridge. Follow this lane until you reach another lane off to the left.

Follow this lane around a 90 degree turn. When this lane reaches a cross road turn left and walk up the hill. At the first gate you come to on the left, slightly set back, cross the stile into this field and walk along the top wall. Just before you would enter a second field you will see a stile and path heading off on your right. Follow the sunken path beyond, keeping straight at any junction. This left footpath will lead you past a house and out onto the main road at Cripplesease.

Once you reach the main road follow it towards St Ives for thirty yards or so until you reach a road off on the right opposite a property called The Wink.

Follow this road taking the first right again. If you choose to shorten your route the path you took should lead you onto this road. Follow it down hill and you will reach the Red River once again. Turn right and return to the village along the road, which you will shortly recognise.

ZENNOR HEAD

START in Zennor village itself. The village boasts a fine public house, The Tinners Arms, a backpackers hostel and cafe which provides walkers with refreshments, and a small Museum.

Before starting your walk take the time to explore the village and especially the Church. From the church gate turn right and walk up the rise towards the village hall. Follow the road around to the left behind the Tinners.

This road will lead all the way along to the old coastguard station, now a private house. Off this road you will find the coast path dipping away to your left into Pendour Cove and beyond.

At the old coastguard station the road ends and picks up the coast path again as you enter the National Trust property of Zennor Head. Follow the path until you reach the headland and its rocky outcrops.

The best time of day to make this walk is late afternoon or a summer's evening when the setting sun bathes the walker in its evening light.

Return the way you came along the path and then the road.

GURNARD'S HEAD

START at the Gurnard's Head Hotel, which lies two miles from Zennor, along the coast road at the hamlet of Treen. Parking is possible on the verge opposite the 'Gurnard's Head'.

From the pub take the road beside the cluster of farm buildings and houses which make up Treen itself. As the houses end a footpath breaks away on the left hand side between a house and its garage. Climb over the stile and follow the path through the fields beyond. From these fields you will be able to see the impressive headland that is Gurnard's Head. The low neck rising to a bulbous head with its resemblance to the Gurnard fish provided the head with its English name and the dark age peoples with an easily defendable cliff castle. As you cross the neck you can easily imagine the rampart-like rocks as castle towers rising above you.

Return the way you came.

LELANT to ST IVES

START at Lelant Church and from here take the footpath over the golf course towards the beach (as in Walk Seven). At the machine-gun pillbox, turn left where the path runs alongside the edge of the course near the railway line. This path then takes you through the sand dunes above Porthkidney Beach, before rising towards Carrack Gladden (Hawke's Point).

Along this path you will pass through Nut Grove. Just past a footpath on the left is a set of steps. At the bottom of these is a small footpath off to the right. This will take you steeply down to a water spring. From the spring site you get an amazing view over Porthkidney. On a summer's day, with an incoming tide over golden sand, this view could be anywhere from Australia to South Africa.

Return to the main footpath again. Just past the railway crossing on your right is a footpath leading off to the right. This path will take you around Carrack Gladden and bring you out on the road above Carbis Bay Beach. Walk down the hill and follow the footpath along the top of the the beach. This footpath leads up the hill beside the Carbis Bay Hotel and will bring you onto Hain Walk, via a railway footbridge. Follow Hain Walk, past the Huer's Hut and down the hill to Porthminster Beach.

HALSETOWN to ST IVES

START at the Halsetown Inn. The inn is on one of the village bus stops – so easy to get to without a car.

Halsetown is a small village which was originally purpose built for the mining community – an early example of 'town planning'.

From the inn walk into the village – away from the main road. Further up the street on your left you will see an old building which was once the village Methodist Chapel. Turn left and head up the road into Polmanter Touring Park. At the end of the first field on your left, where the road bends slightly to the right, you will see a kissing gate with a sign "Footpath to St Ives'. Follow the path through the fields, past a standing stone, and the next road you come to will be Steeple Lane.

Turn left and follow the road down into St Ives. On the right, just past the car park for the Edward Hain Memorial Hospital, turn right down Talland Road. Follow the road down and around until you are facing the doors of some old-fashioned garages. Turn left here and follow the road down, branching off right at a flight of steps and once again you are in St Ives beside the Catholic Church.

HALSETOWN to ST IVES via KNILL'S MONUMENT

START at the Halsetown Inn. From the inn walk into the village (as Walk Twelve). Continue to follow the road past the old Methodist Chapel and up the hill beyond.

As the road starts to descend again you will see Knill's Monument on the top of Worvas Hill ahead of you. As the road bends to the right at the base of the hill strike off left up the St Michael's Way following the signpost to Knill's Monument. Take the first path on the right and follow it to the Monument.

Follow the tarmacked footpath down to Steeple Lane. Return to St Ives via Steeple Lane and the main St Ives road as on Walk Six.

ZENNOR to ST IVES via the FIELD PATH

START at Zennor Church. From here there are two alternative routes – they are both longer and involve more hills! If you turn right and follow the road down to Zennor Head you can then follow the coast path back to St Ives. The second option is to turn left and walk out of the village to the main B3306 coast road. You can then follow this back to St Ives.

The Field Path is a more pleasant option, a picturesque stroll and the least demanding.

From the church wander a few yards up hill to the Village Hall. Beside the wall is a path leading up into the fields. From here you can follow a well sign-posted and stiled path through the fields and farms. Navigation through the farms can be a bit tricky – so keep a look out for the signposts.

The path will lead you from farm to farm through Tremedda, Wicca, Trendrine, Trevega and Trowan until you arrive at Burthallan Lane. For many years this path was the main route to church and work for those living and working on these farms and neighbouring mines.

Once in Burthallan Lane you can turn left and drop down to Clodgy Point and return as Walk Three or turn right and return by reversing Walk Three.

TRENCROM to ST IVES

START at the National Trust car park on the south side of Trencrom Hill. Follow the footpath up onto the summit of the hill and down the footpath, as described in Walk Twenty.

Once you reach the base of the hill, where the woodland starts, off to the left is a footpath with a stile at its end. Cross the stile and the road beyond and into the field. Keep the wall on your right through this field, where at the bottom corner the path leaves it beside the Old Chapel. Follow the path along the property boundry and this will bring you out on the Lelant to Halsetown road.

Turn left and a few yards down the road you will see the National Trust managed curiosity of The Bowl Rock – a large round boulder resting on a small green – said to be the bowling ball of the Giant of Trencrom.

Follow the track to the right of the rock, as you look at it. This will lead you up a driveway to Beersheba Cottage. At the Cottage a hard to find footpath leads up to the right of the property from the back of the small

parking bay. The path runs up between two field walls, over a stile and into a large field with a standing stone. Keep to this field's left hand wall, and continue over a stile in the top corner, into the next field, and along the wall on your right and out into a small lane.

As you cross into this road you will see a farmyard immediately in front of you. Cross the field to the right of the farmyard. Once through this field a footpath crosses a bridleway and into Little Trevarrack Holiday Park.

Follow the park road around to the right and you will see a signpost bearing the yellow arrow marking a footpath. Follow this sign out of the park and along the base of a property into Laity Lane.

Cross the road and take the track opposite. Stick to the right when it narrows and past the first property you next see, when the footpath becomes a driveway, you will find a footpath off to your left.

This footpath will lead you through Carninney Farm and out onto a trackway opposite a horse paddock. Keep this paddock on your right and a few yards up the hill you will see a footpath running along the top of the field. This path will take you to Steeple Lane along the lower edge of the Steeple Woodland Nature Reserve.

Turn right down Steeple Lane and as the woodland on your right ends, and the houses begin, you should see a footpath leading off on your left. Follow this path, which will make a 90 degree turn, before running down beside the St Ives Secondary School.

Once you reach the school road turn left and follow this until the junction where you turn right.

This road will bring you out at the back of the Edward Hain Hospital just after which you turn right and follow Talland Road until you see old-fashioned garages in front of you. Turn left and right again and you will be on the main road into St Ives above Porthminster Beach and near the Malakoff gardens and the main bus station.

Turning left and following this road will bring you to the St Ives Catholic Church at the top of Tregenna Hill.

ZENNOR HILL & QUOIT

START in Zennor village. Opposite the village bus stop is the track leading up Foage Valley. From the bus stop walk back up the hill a short distance towards St Ives until you come to a small footpath leading off landward.

Follow this footpath across Churchtown Common. Above Rosmorran Farm, the first buildings you come to, turn left and head up hill. Once at the top of the hill you will see striking granite outcrops and as you head seaward again along the summit plateau you will see large boulders resting on a platform of golden granite – a wonderful place to be in the early evening on a summer's day. From here you can see the coastline heading towards Pendeen, were the sun will set over the sea.

You will reach a fence line with an iron gate. Once through here turn right and follow the obvious path towards St Ives. When you reach a fork take the right hand track and this will bring you to the collapsed chamber cairn of Zennor Quoit itself.

Leave the Quoit and walk towards the remains of an old mine building to the north of the Quoit. At the ruins turn left onto another path. Once this joins a wide tracked path turn right and head for the main road.

Once you reach the road follow it until you arrive back in Zennor at the bus stop.

ROSEWALL HILL

START at a lay-by on the crest of the ridge between the two hills of Rosewall and Trevalgan on the B3306 coast road. On the St Ives end of the lay-by is a kissing gate, follow the path beyond as it climbs the hill. Go through another gate beside a small quarry and continue up. At a third gate strike off left following a wall.

Past a rocky outcrop you will find a larger path heading along the flat ridge towards St Ives. Follow this, keeping to the higher path, when it narrows. The two paths wander through the broken ground of old opencast and deep mining operations and will lead you onto spoil heaps remaining from 19th and 20th century mining activity. Below you will see two chimney stacks.

Walk to the first chimney stack and follow a path off on the left. This will meet with another track where you turn left again and follow this new path under and then up and around to the back of the large granite outcrop. From here find the small footpath striking off towards the lay-by. This path may take some finding and appear overgrown but it is only a few yards before you reach a gate and the path opens out. This will lead you back to the first gate you went through beside the small quarry.

Return the way you have come, back to the lay-by.

There is much visual evidence in St Ives and the surrounding area of the mining industry which has existed in Cornwall for thousands of years.

It is thought that traders from the Mediterranean visited Cornwall as early as 2,150 BCE, in the early Bronze Age, to buy and trade in tin and other metals. Known to those traders as Cassiterides, or Tin Islands, Cornwall and west Devon provided most of the UK's tin, copper and arsenic until recent times.

Originally found as alluvial deposits in the gravels of stream beds, as tin became harder to find on the surface, or in opencast mines, under ground working began as early as the 16th century.

By the following century mining had begun on Rosewall Hill. In Cyril Noall's 1993 *St Ives Mining District – Vol Two* he describes Rosewall Hill and Ransom United (Goole Pellas) mines as:

> *Among the more picturesque mine remains in the St Ives area are the ruined stacks and engine houses of the old Rosewall Hill and Ransom United mine. This is a very ancient bal; and the eastern side of the hill on which it lies is riddled with old shafts some of which exhibit the most primitive method of working. A zig-zag road runs to the summit to serve some shafts there and it is said that in calm weather the men on night core walking up in procession with their lighted candles in their hats formed a line of moving lights that made a striking appearance against the dark hillside.*

Noall also noted that there is a court record from 1680 which provided very early evidence of mining on the hill. When one James Quicke, of Zennor was giving evidence over Andrew Rosewall's refusal to pay tithes he stated that the defendant:

> *'doth depasture his cattell on the tenement called Rosewall and on that parte of the tenement called Boreesa in the possession of the defendant'*

More importantly he stated that Rosewall did:

> *'likewise keepe and depasture on the said premisses three or ffower labouringe horses Nagges or Mares which the defendant hath from tyme to tyme and doth usually imploy them in carringe of tyn stuffe to the Stampings Mill and allsoe to the bloweinge howse.'*

The hill was in the possession of various mining companies during its time as a producing mine, finally ending up in the hands of the St Ives Consolidated Mines Ltd in 1908.

GEORGIA LAKE – BAKER'S PIT

THIS is possibly the most out of the way walk in this book – but well worth the effort. From where you park (see map) walk though the gate and up the track past the mine engine house. As the track bends to the left you will see a gate on your right. Nip through the gate and down to the lake's edge.

Back on the path a little way above the lake gate is a footpath sign which will lead you through a field at the top of the lake into a more brushy area. Continue through a gate and along the path over a couple of streams, just past the second stream you will see the remains of buildings. Continue up the path through a gate and into an open field to the right. A track leaves the field from the corner of the field closest to the lake. Follow this track onto a flat area below the spoils heaps of granite blocks.

Follow the path to the left running uphill beside the heap. When this becomes a wider track continue up to the quarry gate. To the left here is a well made footpath. Follow this path for quite a long way down to a metal gate. This leads you onto a track. Continue down this track until you reach a stony vehicle track. Turn left and follow this track back to the car.

Just before you arrive at the car you will see, over the fence on your right, the remains of the china clay processing buildings and baths. It is worth finding the path that leads down to these for a look around.

The China Clay industry

The mining, quarrying and general industrial significance of Cornwall really is staggering. A fact recognised by the county's status as a World Heritage Site. Not only is the county famous for its tin, copper and countless other minerals from tungsten to radium but its granite is also some of the finest in the world and its china clay desposit, the largest in the world. Compared to the massive quarries and waste heaps of the St Austell area Baker's Pit is tiny, but of course, no less important – and also a very pleasant walk.

The Cornish china clay deposits have been worked since 1746 with 120 million tons having been extracted. However, reserves are predicted to last at least another hundred years. China clay, or kaolin, itself was used by the Chinese to make a pure white porcelain over a thousand years ago.

In 1768 clay was developed by the Plymouth Porcelain Factory into a fine, genteel white porcelain, instead of the traditional coarse earthenware or stoneware items. Other potteries started to use Cornish china clay, and by the early nineteenth century the kaolin industry had become a major business.

By 1910 production was nearly one million tons a year with the paper industry using more than ceramics, and Cornwall holding a virtual monopoly on world supply.

Baker's is actually the amalgamation of several early pits of the Towednack area, including Bedlam Green, Bohemia, Little Bohemia, Georgia, Little Georgia and Polhigey all of which date to the early 1800s. However, an as yet unidentified pit was described as working as early as 1758.

In 1858 a pit producing 300 tons of potting clay a year was rented to a Mr Truscott by owners Tonkin & Gilbert. Sometime in the late 1860s the works were acquired by William King Baker and Company.

The process of extracting china clay involved removing the clay sand from the pit by means of horse-whim driven rail trucks. It was then pumped through mica drags by the river near the kiln to separate the good from the poor quality clay. The quality clay was then dried in the pan kiln while the poorer, mica-clay, was dried in an open shed.

Baker went into partnership with John and William Lovering, but the works remained in his name and under his management. When he died in 1910 the works were transferred to the Loverings, as Lovering and Pochin Ltd.

The first World War put a temporary stop to the working of the pit which then passed into the hands of the new English China Clays in 1932 and officially closed in 1942.

TRENCROM HILL

START at Trencrom Hill's southern side where there is a car park. From the car park a path climbs the hill past a distinctive boulder perched on an outcrop. As you approach the skyline it is worth imagining the same skyline crowned with a wooden palisade wall – for this hilltop is one of the many hill and cliff forts in the area. As you walk through a gap in the wall, and turn around to view the path you have followed, you will be able to appreciate the views and the geography which appealed to the hill's fort builders. A look to the St Ives side of the hill and you can view the remains of the earthen and stone ramparts.

Take your time to wander the summit platform with its rocky outcrops and tors. Wander down the slope of the plateau and, when you are ready, follow the path leading downwards off the hill's northern end. Take every right fork that presents itself. By doing this the path will lead you around the base of the hill, where you can really appreciate its geography, and back to your start point.

Trencrom Hill, which has also been known as Trecobben Hill, has been the property of the National Trust since 1946 when the land was donated by Lt Col Tyringham as a permanent memorial to the local men and women killed during both world wars.

The hilltop is the site of an Iron age hill fort and, as mentioned, boasts a clearly visible second century BCE rampart. On the summit plateau are also visible the dips which once were round houses. An excellent viewpoint it is also the scene of several local folk stories involving giants and spriggans.

According to legend the hill was home to a race of giants who buried their 'gold and jewels . . . deep in granite caves of this hill'. Secure, even today, from discovery the giants also placed an additional guard on their treasure in the form of the race of 'trolls' known as Spriggans.

In the 1903, third edition, of Robert Hunt's *Popular Romances of the West of England*, he recounts the following local legend:

It is not many years since a man, who thought he was fully informed as to the spot in which a crock of the giant's gold was buried, proceeded on one fine moonlight night to this enchanted hill, and with spade and pick commenced his search.

He proceeded for some time without interruption, and it became evident to him that the treasure was not far off. The sky was rapidly covered with the darkest clouds, shutting out the brilliant light of the moon – which had previously gemmed each cairn – and leaving the gold-seeker in total and unearthly darkness.

The wind rose, and roared terrifically amidst the rocks; but this was soon drowned amidst the fearful crashes of thunder, which followed in quick succession the lashes of lightning. By its light the man perceived that the spriggans were coming out in swarms from all the rocks.

They were in countless numbers; and although they were small at first, they rapidly increased in size, until eventually they assumed an almost giant form, looking all the while, as he afterwards said, 'as ugly as if they would eat him.'

How this poor man escaped is unknown, but he is said to have been so frightened that he took to his bed, and was not able to work for a long time.

DYNAMITE QUAY & HAYLE ESTUARY

START at Lelant Church, where there is a small lay-by and further roadside parking. Walk away from the church with your back to it and turn left following the road down the hill. This road will bring you to a rail platform and old station house.

From the station continue along the road, over a small bridge and onto a straight section of road. At the end of this section, where the road turns 90 degrees to the right, a small cut through path heads off left into the Park & Ride. Turn right and walk out of the Park & Ride through the housing estate of Saltings Reach.

Turn left and walk along the road to the Old Quay House public house. A suitable rest stop at the half-way point. Be careful here as there is no pavement along this section of the walk. Once past the Quay House you are on the causeway with the estuary mud flats to your left and the RSPB reserve of Ryan's Field, with its prominent hide, on the right of the road.

Follow this road all the way into Hayle. Just before you reach the viaduct turn left and walk along the path which runs beside the viaduct between its towers and the harbour. Turn left along Penpol Terrace with its traditionally fronted shops. Continue past the Royal Standard public house and on the left a metal bridge crosses the sluice gate which once allowed the Harbour Master to naturally control the build up of sand in the estuary's channel by periodically releasing water from Copperhouse Pool. In conjunction with the release of water from Carnsew Pool – a section of the estuary – this rush of water sluiced out any build-up without the need for expensive dredging.

Cross the bridge and keep the harbour and estuary on your left and follow the road. Near the slipway you will see old industrial rail tracks embedded in the road. Follow these rails until you reach the end of the road when it branches into two. The right branch will be heading up hill. In front of you will be the derelict buildings which were once the coal-fired power station. Take the left branch of the road – the un-tarmacked branch. Follow this up to the car park and the sand cliffs overlooking St Ives Bay.

This is the end of the walk. Return the way you came or return to Hayle where a bus stop is situated opposite the sluice gate bridge.

SUGGESTIONS

I HOPE you've enjoyed these short walks around the wonderful area of St Ives and its bay. The walks took you through some wonderful scenery and hopefully opened up further vistas for you. Here are a couple of extensions to the walks described and one or two further afield walks.

The Gurnard's and Zennor Head walks can be linked together. From Treen walk to Gurnard's Head as described. Once you leave the headland stick to the lower path off to the left. This is the coastpath and by following it you will arrive at Zennor Head, near the Old Coastguard Station. You can then follow the road up into the village. Go past the Wayside Museum and out of the village. Follow the road towards Gurnard's Head and along here you will find signposts marking the continuation of the field path. This field path will take you back to the Gurnard's Head Hotel, where you parked.

Another option would be the coastpath from Zennor to St Ives. Follow the walk as for Zennor Head and simply follow the signs to St Ives. Be warned this is about five miles of surprisingly hard walking, with more ups and downs than you might expect. The most often heard comment from people who have done this section is: 'I didn't expect it to be *that* hard.' But it is worth the effort.

A final link up could see you walking from Trencrom to St Ives, via Halsetown. Follow the guide as the Trencrom to St Ives walk, but once you go through Little Trevarrack Holiday Park and hit the road turn left and follow this road all the way into Halsetown.

If you have done either of the Halsetown to St Ives walks you will recognise the road so you may choose to either turn off up to Knill's Monument or up into Polmanter for the field path walk.

Some more titles from

THE ST IVES PRINTING & PUBLISHING COMPANY
High Street, St Ives, Cornwall, TR26 1RS (01736) 795813

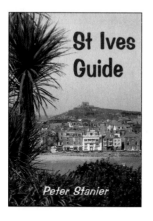

ST IVES GUIDE

ST IVES GUIDE was first published in 2004 and has proved popular ever since.

Drawing on his knowledge of the town author Peter Stanier has produced a book full of interesting facts and tit-bits about St Ives, its past, geology, institutions, people and its customs.

St Ives Guide
author: Peter Stanier; photographs: Tobi Carver

HEADLAND WALKS – ST IVES to SENNEN

ST IVES TO SENNEN is the first book published in the Headland Walks Series by author Peter Stanier.

First published in 2005 the author takes you on ten walks around notable headlands on the north Penwith coast: from St Ives' Island, to the cliff castle headlands of Bosigran, Gurnard's Head and Kenidjack to Sennen itself.

Headland Walks – St Ives to Sennen
author: Peter Stanier; photographs: Tobi Carver

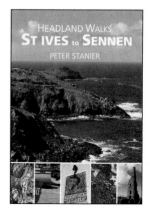

HEADLAND WALKS –
LAND'S END TO TREWAVAS HEAD

LAND'S END TO TREWAVAS HEAD is the second in the Headland Walks Series by author Peter Stanier.

First published in 2008 ten more walks continue around notable headlands on the south Penwith coast from Land's End to the historic Wireless Point and on to Trewavas Head and its remnants of the mining industry.

Headland Walks – Land's End to Trewavas Head
author: Peter Stanier; photographs: Tobi Carver